POST AND PARK

SAN FRANCISCO

N

POST AND PARK

A BRIEF ILLUSTRATED HISTORY
OF THE PRESIDIO OF SAN FRANCISCO

BY *Stephen A. Haller*

GOLDEN GATE NATIONAL PARKS ASSOCIATION
SAN FRANCISCO, CALIFORNIA

COVER: THE 51ST IOWA VOLUNTEER INFANTRY REGIMENT MARCHES THOUGH THE PRESIDIO'S LOMBARD STREET GATE IN 1898, BOUND FOR MANILA.

INSIDE FRONT COVER, P. I: MAP ADAPTED FROM "SAN FRANCISCO EARTHQUAKE/ REPORT ON WATERWORKS APRIL 18, 1906," USED WITH PERMISSION OF THE SAN FRANCISCO HISTORY CENTER, SAN FRANCISCO PUBLIC LIBRARY.

FRONTIS (P. II): *THE GOLDEN GATE BEFORE THE BRIDGE, SAN FRANCISCO, CALIFORNIA, 1932* ©1995 BY THE TRUSTEES OF THE ANSEL ADAMS PUBLISHING RIGHTS TRUST. ALL RIGHTS RESERVED.

———————

OUR THANKS TO THE NPS/GOLDEN GATE NATIONAL RECREATION AREA CURATORIAL STAFF FOR THEIR HELP IN LOCATING HISTORICAL PHOTOGRAPHS, AND TO OTHER NPS INTERPRETIVE AND RESOURCE MANAGEMENT STAFF FOR THEIR INTEREST AND SUGGESTIONS.

———————

EDITOR: SUSAN TASAKI
DESIGNER: JAMISON SPITTLER
PRODUCTION ASSISTANTS:
DIANA S. LARRIMORE, VICKIE HO
PRINTED ON RECYCLED PAPER IN HONG KONG THROUGH GLOBAL INTERPRINT, INC.

For my mom and dad

Library of Congress Catalog Card Number 96-78727

ISBN 1-883869-23-4

Ansel Adams Publishing Rights Trust, pages ii, 36
Bancroft Library, page 24
Ernest Braun, page 32
Charles Kennard, pages 22, 35, 38, back cover
Middleton/Liittschwager, page 37
National Japanese American Historical Society, page 30
Anthony Powell, page 27
Cindy Ellen Russell, page 41

CONTENTS

1599. BRICK BARRACKS, AND HDQ'RS., PRESIDIO, AND S.F. BAY,

THE MAIN POST OF THE PRESIDIO, CIRCA 1905. *(Photograph courtesy PARC/GGNRA)*

The Presidio tells the story of the development of the western United States, and its growth from an isolated frontier into a gateway to the nations of the Pacific.

By nearly any measure, the Presidio of San Francisco is a military post of exceptional significance. Its association with a wide spectrum of historical events helps educate us about the development of the American West, helps us understand who we are, and provides a frame of reference within which to contemplate the future. Part of the Golden Gate National Recreation Area, designated in its own right as a National Historic Landmark (the highest form of recognition this nation can give to a historic property), the post is a rich and complex mix of buildings and landscape that preserves the feeling of the past in a setting of spectacular natural beauty. The Presidio's significance comes not only from the resources within its boundaries, but also from its location, guarding one of the world's finest natural harbors and surrounded by the densely populated city of San Francisco. The Presidio possesses in abundance those traditional values of historic significance, ecological richness, and splendid vistas that earn it a place in our very special National Park system.

The longest-lived Army installation in the American West, and one of the longest-garrisoned posts in the country, the Presidio reflects more than 200 years of military history under three flags.

In 1776, the same year the Declaration of Independence was signed in Philadelphia, a remarkable overland expedition led by Lieutenant Colonel Juan Bautista de Anza trekked northward from Sonora, Mexico, on the far western side of the continent. These simultaneous events might just as well have occurred at opposite ends of the world, yet within the span of a lifetime, the young United States had spread across North America and encompassed the Hispanic settlement on the Pacific Coast's finest harbor. Some considered such expansion to be "Manifest Destiny." Regardless of the justification, this westward expansion helped assure that the United States would eventually become a world power.

Recognizing the strategic importance of the great harbor named for St. Francis, Spanish colonial officials ordered a new *presidio*, or fortified garrison, to be established on the northern California frontier. Anza led 240 men, women, and children and 1,000 head of livestock across the southwestern deserts and mountains to San Francisco Bay. Upon reaching their destination, Father Pedro Font described the "port" of San Francisco as "a marvel of nature, and might well be called a harbor of harbors because of its great capacity, and of several small bays which it unfolds in its margins or beach and in its islands."

The military garrison established here marked the northernmost permanent frontier of Spain's New World empire. From this spot, four missions, two villages, and a royal rancho were founded. While Franciscan missionaries at the nearby Mission San Francisco de Asis proselytized among the resident Native Americans, persuading or coercing them into changing from their traditional ways to those of Catholicism, Presidio troops protected the priests and mounted a number of military and exploratory expeditions that penetrated far inland.

Beginning in the 1790s, the narrow harbor entrance was fortified with a dozen guns mounted behind adobe walls, initiating two centuries of heavy artillery guarding the Golden Gate. The isolated garrison was a small token of Spain's claim to the realm, but the symbolism of the royal flag gave the competing colonial powers of Russia and Great Britain cause to hesitate—attempts to seize the Presidio could touch off a European war.

By the time the Spanish garrison accepted the new authority of Mexico in 1822, the Presidio was in decline. Troop strength dwindled as soldiers left for life in the nearby civilian settlement of Yerba Buena (later known as San Francisco), and the silent cannon rested on rotting carriages at the fort overlooking the Gate. But evidence of the post's Hispanic heritage remains. The Officers' Club contains adobe walls,

THE ROYAL SPANISH COAT-OF-ARMS REPRESENTS THE ANCIENT KINGDOMS OF CASTILE AND LEON. IT SYMBOLIZES SPANISH RULE IN THE 18TH CENTURY, AND REMAINED THE POST'S CREST UNTIL THE U.S. ARMY LEFT IN THE 20TH CENTURY.
(Illustration courtesy PARC/GGNRA)

and the foundations of the early Presidio lie just underfoot. Six bronze cannon from the fort, the oldest dated fortress artillery in the nation, are located on the post. These guns were captured during the Bear Flag Revolt of 1846, when California passed from Mexico to the United States. One of the cannon still has the spike blocking its touchhole left by the landing party that disabled it, a party led by famed explorer John C. Fremont and mountain man "Kit" Carson.

When the great Gold Rush of 1849 created a legendary boom in California, the U.S. government turned its attention to protecting the strategic harbor. A state-of-the-art brick fortress slowly arose at the location of the old Spanish battery, and was called Fort Point. It remains the only classic "third-system" fort ever built on the West Coast of the United States. However, the Presidio proper languished. Army officers soon to make their mark in the Civil War commanded here—men such as Erasmus D. Keyes, Lewis Armistead, and E. O.C Ord—yet post improvements were not made. Meanwhile, expensive harbor fortifications were built, and the soldiers deserted in droves for the gold fields. A visiting officer noted that "the view of the Bay is fine from the high hills, but everything looks dirty and sandy; you cannot avoid the impression that it is a mean country."

In 1861, the outbreak of the Civil War changed everything. The state, with its gold mines, quicksilver deposits, and access to the silver of the Comstock Lode, became one of the Union's essential assets. In the eyes of strategists, the Presidio and the fort at Fort Point were bastions against the Confederacy's schemes for California and the Pacific

Coast. It wasn't long before the post began to develop from a ramshackle frontier outpost to a military establishment that resembled its counterparts elsewhere in the nation. As a measure of the post's importance, the 9th U.S. Infantry Regiment, assigned to service on the Pacific Coast, was headquartered at the Presidio; it was one of the few Regular Army regiments not called east to fight.

In addition to the well-preserved fort at Fort Point overlooking the harbor entrance, the heart of today's main post preserves the spirit of the 1860s in its buildings, street grid, and landscapes. A row of officers' family houses lining the east side of the old parade ground was, for many years, the largest such row at any permanent military post west of the Mississippi. Considered collectively with the fort, these houses, the garrison chapel, the powder magazine, post hospital, and wagon and quartermaster buildings represent the most substantial Civil War-era military complex in the Far West.

Once the crisis of the Civil War had passed, the Presidio took on an increasingly important role in the settlement and growth of the Western frontier. Emboldened by the diversion of military strength to the great conflict in the East, western tribes redoubled their efforts to drive out settlers and preserve their ways of life. The expanded post became a central deployment point for forces engaged in the Indian Wars throughout the West. As early as 1858, troops from the Presidio had been sent to war against

JOHN CHARLES FREMONT, "THE PATHFINDER" WHO NAMED THE GOLDEN GATE.

THE AMERICAN FLAG WAS RAISED OVER THE PRESIDIO IN 1847, YET THE POST CHANGED VERY LITTLE FROM MEXICAN DAYS UNTIL THE CIVIL WAR. *(Both illustrations courtesy PARC/GGNRA)*

THE PRESIDIO.

THE CLASSIC BRICK FORTRESS AT FORT POINT, THE ONLY ONE OF ITS KIND ON THE WEST COAST, WAS RUSHED TO COMPLETION AT THE ONSET OF THE CIVIL WAR; PHOTOGRAPH CIRCA 1869.

(Photograph courtesy PARC/GGNRA)

the Spokane tribe of eastern Washington; in 1860, they rode against the Paiute tribe of Nevada. In 1872, the Presidio's 4th Artillery marched to northern California and fierce conflict with the Modoc tribe in the Lava Beds. In one ambush alone, twenty Presidio soldiers died; the Modocs disappeared with their casualties into a wilderness of rocks. Troops from the Presidio garrison pursued the Nez Perce in Idaho Territory under Brigadier General O. O. Howard, fought the Bannocks in Oregon, and campaigned with Brigadier General George Crook against Geronimo's Apaches in Arizona.

While Presidio troops marched and fought across the Far West, the post itself became headquarters for the Military Division of the Pacific under such notable commanders as Major General Irvin McDowell and Major General John Pope. One of the Army's leading strategic and tactical theorists, Colonel Emory Upton, served as post commander, and his tenure firmly links the Presidio with the movement to modernize the U.S. Army in the late nineteenth century.

This trend towards modernization is one of the great changes in the turn-of-the-century U.S. Army as represented by the Presidio. As the country was settled and the Indian Wars came to an end, the Army evolved from a frontier constabulary to a modern institution of international power. Remote frontier outposts closed, and fewer but larger posts were created near major railheads and seaports. This movement is clearly reflected at the Presidio by the massive concrete coast artillery emplacements that ring the shoreline of the Golden Gate. These heavy-caliber batteries formed one of the most up-to-date coastal defense sys-

FREDERICK FUNSTON EARNED THE MEDAL OF HONOR DURING THE PHILIPPINE INSURRECTION FOR HIS DARING BEHIND-THE-LINES MISSION TO CAPTURE THE NATIONALIST LEADER EMILIO AGUINALDO. HE IS ALSO NOTABLE FOR HIS LEADERSHIP OF ARMY RELIEF EFFORTS IN THE WAKE OF THE GREAT SAN FRANCISCO EARTHQUAKE AND FIRE OF 1906.

(Photograph courtesy PARC/GGNRA)

tems in the country, and now constitute a fine outdoor museum of sea-coast artillery. They are tangible manifestations of the nation's entry onto the stage of world power and international involvement.

The Spanish-American War of 1898 focused national attention on the Presidio as the principal marshaling area for troops bound for the Philippines, and presaged a century of increasing American involvement with the affairs of Asia and the Pacific—a theme as relevant today as it was then. The Presidio is one of the finest places in the United States to gain a perspective on this watershed in American history.

In the aftermath of the great San Francisco earthquake and fire of 1906, troops from the Presidio helped restore order in the city, while the Army Hospital and the post as a whole provided shelter and relief services for the citizens of San Francisco. This effort established the post's continuing role in providing aid to the civilian community, a role furthered by work done on the Presidio by agencies such as the Works Progress Administration and the Civilian Conservation Corps during the 1930s. (Disaster assistance remained a mission of the Sixth U.S. Army until base closure in 1994.)

Aside from sending existing garrison units to fight in Europe, the Presidio contributed to the nation's World War I involvement in three major ways. It served in the training and mobilization of troops; housed and operated a massive officer training camp, creating many new junior officers who left for the front in 1917 and 1918; and, at Letterman Army Hospital, pioneered the Army's use of women as nurses and its application of physical therapy to rehabilitate the wounded.

WHILE IN COMMAND OF THE 8TH INFANTRY BRIGADE AT THE PRESIDIO, JOHN J. PERSHING SUFFERED GREAT TRAGEDY. IN 1915, HIS WIFE AND THREE DAUGHTERS DIED IN A FIRE THAT SWEPT THROUGH THEIR QUARTERS. THE SITE, NOW MARKED BY THE POST'S MAIN FLAG POLE, IS NAMED PERSHING SQUARE.

(Photograph courtesy PARC/GGNRA)

THE 51ST IOWA VOLUNTEER INFANTRY REGIMENT MARCHES THOUGH THE PRESIDIO'S LOMBARD STREET GATE IN 1898, BOUND FOR MANILA. *(Photograph courtesy PARC/GGNRA)*

THE AIRCRAFT OF THE 91ST OBSERVATION SQUADRON ALONG THE FLIGHT LINE AT CRISSY FIELD, FACING THE U.S. COAST GUARD STATION AND THE GOLDEN GATE, 1923. *(Photograph courtesy Dora Devol Brett Collection/PARC/GGNRA)*

The Presidio became headquarters for the 9th Corps Area in 1920 and the Fourth U.S. Army in 1933. Thus it became responsible for military operations in eight western states, geographically just short of one-third of the nation. Additionally, Fort Winfield Scott in the western Presidio continued as headquarters for the Harbor Defenses of San Francisco.

From 1921 to 1936, the operations of the Coast Defense Air Station at Crissy Field placed the Presidio firmly at the forefront in the use of airpower in military operations. Indeed, important milestones in the development of the nation's civilian and aviation infrastructure occurred at Crissy Field. The airfield was built under the supervision of Henry H. "Hap" Arnold, who was destined to lead the Army Air Forces in World War II and to set global strategy as a member of the Joint Chiefs of Staff. The first "dawn-to-dusk" transcontinental flight ended at Crissy Field in 1924, and the first successful round-the-world flight stopped here that same year. When two Navy seaplanes unsuccessfully attempted to fly to Hawaii from Crissy Field, outspoken Assistant Chief of the Air Service "Billy" Mitchell burst out in anger. His remarks precipitated his notorious court martial for insubordination and led to a reexamination of the state of the nation's aviation.

Crissy Field pilots perfected the use of airplanes to correct coast artillery fire, performed aerial photography throughout the West, and searched for fires in the national forests. Crissy Field was the only Army airfield in continuous operation in the western states during these explosive years of maturing of air power, and is the only remaining Coast Defense Air Station in the nation.

MEN OF THE 30TH U.S. INFANTRY REGIMENT POSE IN FRONT OF THEIR BARRACKS ON MONTGOMERY STREET, CIRCA 1915. *(Photograph courtesy PARC/GGNRA)*

THE MEN OF THE 91ST OBSERVATION SQUADRON AND THEIR DE HAVILLAND
BI-PLANES IN FORMATION AT CRISSY FIELD, WITH THE AIRFIELD BARRACKS,
HEADQUARTERS, AND HANGARS IN THE BACKGROUND. THESE ADVENTUROUS

ARMY AVIATORS OF THE 1920S, WHO WERE EXPECTED TO "FLY THEIR OLD
CRATES INTO THE LIMELIGHT," SET NUMEROUS CROSS-COUNTRY AND TRANS-
PACIFIC RECORDS IN CARRYING OUT THEIR ORDERS. *(Photograph courtesy
PARC/GGNRA)*

THE PUBLIC TURNED OUT TO WATCH A PRACTICE FIRING AT BATTERY GODFREY; COMPLETED IN 1895, IT GUARDED THE GOLDEN GATE UNTIL 1943. *(Photograph courtesy PARC/GGNRA)*

Years of mounting tension with Japan and the rise of the Axis powers during the 1930s translated into stepped-up training, including practice in amphibious landings on the Presidio's shore by the 30th U.S. Infantry Regiment, which went on to achieve a distinguished combat record in World War II.

After the bombing of Pearl Harbor in December 1941, Lieutenant General John L. DeWitt assumed responsibility for the defense of the West Coast against a much-feared Japanese attack. The implementation of Executive Order 9066, requiring the relocation and internment of all persons of Japanese ancestry, was carried out under the supervision of the Western Defense Command at the Presidio, even as Japanese-American soldiers trained in secret at the post's Military Intelligence Service Language School. The harbor defenses of San Francisco Bay were commanded for the duration from Fort Winfield Scott. And Letterman Army Hospital became the busiest stateside debarkation hospital of the war.

In the aftermath of World War II, delegates from Australia, New Zealand, and the United States signed a joint security alliance (the ANZUS Pact) at the post's Non-Commissioned Officers' and Enlisted Service Club. A week later, the Joint Security Pact between the United States and Japan was signed there as well. On the same day, September 8, 1951, the official peace treaty formally ending World War II was signed at San Francisco's War Memorial Opera House. Nearly fifty years of hostility between the two superpowers of the Pacific basin had come full circle, and it is fair to say that a new era of international affairs began here.

SECRETARY OF STATE DEAN ACHESON (IMMEDIATE RIGHT) AND SPECIAL AMBASSADOR JOHN FOSTER DULLES (IMMEDIATE LEFT) OBSERVE JAPANESE PREMIER SHIGERU YOSHIDA SIGNING THE JOINT SECURITY PACT AT THE PRESIDIO'S ENLISTED SERVICE CLUB, 1951.
(Photograph courtesy PARC/GGNRA)

AN EVOLVING LANDSCAPE

The Presidio landscape represents an environmental evolution from its natural state to its present scenic and complex cultural landscape.

The location of the Presidio is intimately related to the spectacular geography of the Golden Gate at the entrance to San Francisco Bay. Humans have altered the landscape of the Presidio over the years, enhancing its role as the guardian of the bay, reflecting changing military technology and mission, and making it a more desirable and attractive place to live and work. By preserving the cultural landscape of the Presidio, we provide ourselves and future generations with an internationally recognized example of the evolving influence of humankind on the natural and constructed environment.

The tule-lined shore of Mountain Lake and the spring-fed waters of Lobos Creek running into the sea at Baker Beach recall the natural landscape. Before Europeans came, Native Americans camped in the area gathering reeds for shelter and basketmaking, acorns in the riparian oak woods, and shellfish along the bounteous shoreline.

In the process of colonization, Spanish soldiers and settlers introduced annual grasses, cut brush and trees along the watercourses for firewood, and brought cattle and horses that overgrazed the grasslands. Yet their impact on the environment was relatively small, for they constructed their fortified garrison largely within a three-hundred-yard-square enclosure of adobe walls, linking it by simple paths to the mission and the coastal fortress at the harbor's entrance. It is said that the oldest travel route still existing in San Francisco follows the pathway from the adobe Presidio to the Mission Dolores.

The Civil War reshaped the Presidio into what became the conventional mold of the Victorian-era United States Army post, complete with a central parade ground surrounded by rows of enlisted men's barracks and a separate, distinctive "officers' row," the finest Civil War-era streetscape in San Francisco.

By the 1870s and 1880s, aesthetic concerns were for the first time a major impetus in the development of the post. When the Presidio became the headquarters of the Military Division of the Pacific, housing and landscaping were upgraded to reflect the post's increased stature, and its design deliberately responded to the rolling terrain and scenic views.

As the city of San Francisco began to reach out around the Presidio, ambitious plans were initiated that would forever transform its lands into a parklike and forested reserve. The 1883 Presidio landscape plan duplicated in many ways the design for

"We ascended a small hill and then entered upon a mesa that was very green and flower-covered, with an abundance of wild violets . . . Indeed, although in all my travels I saw very good sites and beautiful country, I saw none which pleased me so much as this. And I think that if it could be well settled like Europe there would not be anything more beautiful in all the world, for it has the best advantages for founding in it a most beautiful city."
— Father Pedro Font,
at the site of the Presidio, 1776

QUARTERS OCCUPIED BY MAJORS AND COLONELS WERE BUILT TO FOLLOW THE CURVE

OF THE HILLSIDE OVERLOOKING LETTERMAN HOSPITAL GROUNDS AND THE PALACE

OF FINE ARTS. *(Photograph courtesy PARC/GGNRA)*

> "The main idea is, to crown the ridges, border the boundary fences, and cover the areas of sand and marsh waste with a forest that will generally seem continuous, and thus appear immensely larger than it really is. By leaving the valleys uncovered or with a scattering fringe of trees along the streams, the contrast of height will be strengthened... in order to make the contrast from the city seem as great as possible, and indirectly accentuate the idea of the power of the government."
>
> — Major W. A. Jones, Division Engineer, Military Division of the Pacific, 1883

Golden Gate Park, and owed much to the influence of noted landscape architects Andrew Jackson Downing or Frederick Law Olmsted, who designed New York City's grand Central Park. (When the first national cemetery on the West Coast was established here in 1884, it too was laid out to take full advantage of the Presidio's hilly topography and magnificent vistas.)

By the end of the century, nearly 100,000 trees had been planted in carefully chosen plots across the post: it was the first large-scale landscaping effort of its type at any Army base. This transformation of the mostly open land into a formal tree-covered environment ranks as a monumental undertaking and as one of the Army's most impressive accomplishments in the area of landscape planning. The Presidio clearly stands apart from all other military installations in the nation as a pioneer in landscape architecture on a massive scale. The wooded, parklike character of the Presidio, conceived in the 1880s, continues to the present day.

The Presidio's spectacular natural setting contributes immeasurably to the overall harmony of its buildings with the landscape. To an extent unusual on military posts, the layout of the post's streets and the position of its buildings were influenced by terrain, conforming to natural contours rather than following rectilinear grids.

In the 1890s, as the Army continued to expand the post, its architects chose materials and styles that would convey a sense of permanence. Brick, stone, and concrete were used for the construction of Colonial Revival residences and barracks, such as the imposing row along Montgomery Street. These solid new buildings, designed in a

THESE WOOD-FRAME OFFICERS' QUARTERS WERE BUILT DURING THE CIVIL WAR. IN THE 1880S, THEY WERE REORIENTED AWAY FROM THE PARADE GROUND TO FACE THE CITY OF SAN FRANCISCO—A MANIFESTATION OF THE ARMY'S DESIRE TO PRESENT AN ELEGANT FACADE TO THE CITY THAT WAS BEGINNING TO SURROUND IT. *(Photograph courtesy PARC/GGNRA)*

THIS MODERN PHOTOGRAPH SHOWS THE MATURE PRESIDIO FOREST, WHICH CONSISTS LARGELY OF STANDS OF EUCALYPTUS, MONTEREY CYPRESS, AND MONTEREY PINE PLANTED NEAR THE TURN OF THE CENTURY, FROM 1886 TO 1906. *(Photograph courtesy Charles Kennard)*

manner that evoked a pride in the past, were intended to manifest the Army's unyielding presence and power. Indeed, the post is a veritable architectural and landscaping layercake.

Experts have observed that the Presidio has a greater variety of buildings and structures than any other Army post in the United States, and constitutes a true "museum" of U.S. Army architecture from 1853 through the 1940s. Some buildings are significant because they so well represent a typical military post, while others are notable as unusual departures from the norm. For example, by the time the United States entered World War II in 1941, an emergency construction program had already covered portions of the Presidio with the ubiquitous mobilization-type wood frame buildings, examples of which remain to this day near the main parade ground. The first use of the distinctive Mission Revival style on an Army base was the Presidio's Fort Winfield Scott, while the last complex of brick stables built by the Army is situated in a secluded vale and reflects the transition from horse to motor power.

———— ❧ ————

RIGHT: PASSING OVER THE POST, AND LINKING IT TO THE REST OF GOLDEN GATE NATIONAL RECREATION AREA, THE GOLDEN GATE BRIDGE FIRMLY ASSOCIATED THE PRESIDIO WITH A VISTA RECOGNIZABLE ALL OVER THE WORLD. CONSTRUCTION OF THE BRIDGE AND ITS APPROACHES, WHICH BEGAN IN 1933, REQUIRED THE COOPERATION OF THE ARMY TO BUILD ON PRESIDIO LAND. *(Photograph courtesy PARC/GGNRA)*

THIS DRAWING OF NATIVE AMERICANS IN THEIR TULE REED BOAT IS THOUGHT TO HAVE BEEN
MADE BY GEORG VON LANGSDORFF, DOCTOR AND NATURALIST ABOARD THE RUSSIAN SHIP *JUNO*,
CIRCA 1806. NOTE THE SPANISH PRESIDIO IN THE BACKGROUND. *(Courtesy the Bancroft Library)*

Throughout its long history, the Presidio has been a cultural crossroads.

From its prominent position at the Golden Gate, the Presidio has played an important part in the rise of San Francisco, the cultural evolution of California, the settlement of the American West, and the involvement of the United States in the international affairs of the Pacific basin.

⸺⸺

The first recorded cross-cultural contact at the Presidio began a process which resulted in the substantial replacement of the traditional Native American way of life with that of the Spanish colonizers and missionaries. Yet the extensive natural areas of the post hold evidence of Native American lifeways and provide rich opportunities to reexamine this early clash of cultures.

It seems impossible to probe anywhere around the main post and not come across buried remains of the old presidio that is the birthplace of San Francisco as we know it today. Extensive archeological investigation has uncovered foundations of Spanish- and Mexican-era buildings and defensive walls extending over an area three times greater than historical records indicated. These structural remains, and artifacts such as tableware, floor tile, and animal bone, provide an alternative textbook with which to interpret the daily activity of the early colonists and the physical environment in which they lived.

NEARLY A DOZEN SHIPWRECKS LIE BURIED ALONG THE PRESIDIO SHORE, A SMALL REFLECTION OF THE VOLUME AND SCOPE OF COMMERCE PASSING THROUGH THE GOLDEN GATE. THIS IS THE NEW ENGLAND-BUILT *FRANK JONES*, WHICH DRIFTED ASHORE JUST SOUTH OF FORT POINT IN 1877. *(Photograph courtesy PARC/GGNRA)*

The textbook's next chapter was written in gold. The Gold Rush of 1849 has been called the greatest mass migration since the Crusades. Suddenly, people from all over the United States, Europe, Asia, indeed from every corner of the world, poured into California, bringing dramatically different ways of life to San Francisco and opening up the floodgates of settlement throughout the Pacific slope. The area's rapid growth and mushrooming commercial and strategic importance spurred the U.S. government to begin a series of fortifications to protect the commerce of this world-renowned port. The establishment of a rescue station of the U.S. Lifesaving Service along the Presidio shoreline and the buried remains of sailing ships from far reaches of the world that lie beneath the Presidio's beaches are less visible but equally dramatic evidence of the area's economic value.

Presidio soldiers also reflected some of the diversity of American society. Elements of all four of the old Army's black regiments, the famed "Buffalo Soldiers" renowned for their bravery, were stationed at the Presidio. Indeed, it was the black soldiers of the 9th U.S. Cavalry who supported Teddy Roosevelt's Rough Riders in the charge up San Juan Hill in Cuba during the Spanish-American War. The same 9th Cavalry of the Presidio garrison provided an honor guard for President Roosevelt when he visited the post in 1903. That year, Captain Charles Young, one of the Army's few black officers, led a troop of Buffalo Soldiers from the Presidio to Sequoia National Park where they completed the road up to the Giant Forest. For the duration of the summer, Young was the new park's acting superintendent.

CAPTAIN CHARLES YOUNG, TAKEN AT THE PRESIDIO IN 1903. A MEMBER OF THE PRESIDIO GARRISON, HE WAS THE THIRD AFRICAN-AMERICAN TO GRADUATE FROM WEST POINT.
(Photograph courtesy Anthony Powell)

The Presidio is an excellent place to interpret the nation's transition from a New World frontier to an international power with responsibilities across the Pacific. The Spanish-American War in 1898 resulted in the U.S. acquisition of Guam and its retention of the Philippines. The latter action brought on the Philippine Insurrection of 1899-1902, a brutal guerilla war that presaged the Vietnam conflict. In 1898, the United States annexed Hawaii; that same year, the Alaska Gold Rush began. The Boxer Rebellion of 1900 led to the stationing of U.S. troops on mainland China until the beginning of World War II. The opening of the Panama Canal in 1914 further increased American involvement in the Pacific Basin. All these developments were linked to the Presidio and were reflected by the expansion and greatly increased levels of activity at the base; a constant stream of troops came to and left from the Presidio, shuttling between the mainland U.S. and the new Pacific possessions. These changes resulted in an increased American presence throughout the Pacific, cross-cultural exchange, and vibrant multiethnic communities on the West Coast.

Not all of these exchanges were positive, but all provided lessons to ponder. One of the most relevant and poignant is the relationship of the Presidio to Japanese-American history during World War II. In 1942, security concerns, wartime hysteria, and racial prejudice resulted in Executive Order 9066. This required the evacuation of all Americans of Japanese ancestry from the West Coast, and the Headquarters of the Western Defense Command at the Presidio took the lead in directing the relocation and internment effort. Considerably easier to access than the sites of the notorious "relocation" camps, the Presidio illuminates this dark chapter of our history.

PRESIDENT THEODORE ROOSEVELT (HATLESS IN CARRIAGE, LOWER LEFT) VISITED THE PRESIDIO IN 1903.
NOTE THE BUFFALO SOLDIERS OF THE 9TH U.S. CAVALRY IN HIS ESCORT. *(Photograph courtesy PARC/GGNRA)*

It is ironic that Japanese-American soldiers in Army uniform labored at their studies at the Presidio's Military Intelligence Service Language School while their families were being interned. At the school, Japanese-American soldiers learned translation and battlefield interrogation skills that enabled them to save countless Allied lives and perhaps shorten the war—they proved their loyalty, but their story was veiled in military secrecy for nearly fifty years.

Indeed, the Army itself as a community was reflected in the lives of the thousands of soldiers and their families who lived on the post and made careers here. Childhood experienced in a military environment and the changing role of women on a military post are but two of the Presidio's many narrative threads. As one Presidio officer put it, "I do not think we should miss sight of the fact that we. . . live in time of peace [for] many years, waiting for possible wartime developments."

The distance from the environment that the Native Americans knew to the urban setting of today's Presidio is great. Yet the complex mix of cultures that has characterized this nation from the days of colonial expansion and Manifest Destiny to the present unfolds for us at the Presidio.

LEFT: THE U.S. ARMY'S FIRST INTELLIGENCE LANGUAGE SCHOOL TRAINED JAPANESE-AMERICAN SOLDIERS IN A FORMER AIR MAIL HANGAR AT CRISSY FIELD, 1941-1942. THIS MODEST FACILITY EVENTUALLY EVOLVED INTO THE DEFENSE LANGUAGE INSTITUTE. *(Photograph courtesy the National Japanese American Historical Society)*

THESE HAPPY FACES BELONG TO THE CHILDREN OF AVIATORS "HAP" ARNOLD, GEORGE BRETT, AND ROBERT SELFF. THE PHOTOGRAPH WAS TAKEN IN THE 1920S IN FRONT OF THE LINCOLN BOULEVARD QUARTERS ASSIGNED TO CRISSY FIELD OFFICERS. *(Photograph courtesy Dora Devol Brett Collection/PARC/GGNRA)*

THE PRESIDIO IS BORDERED ON THE WEST BY THE WATERS OF THE PACIFIC OCEAN, ON THE NORTH BY

SAN FRANCISCO BAY, AND ON THE SOUTH AND EAST BY THE URBAN LANDSCAPE OF SAN FRANCISCO.

(Photograph courtesy Ernest Braun)

The Presidio provides an island of refuge for nature in an urban environment.

Early naturalists accompanying European explorers calling at San Francisco Bay were the first to scientifically describe some of the Presidio's most notable species. Adelbert von Chamisso and Johann Friedrich Eschscholtz, aboard the Russian brig *Ruik*, first named and identified many of today's well-known native plants, including the California poppy, *Eschscholzia californica*, from specimens collected at the Presidio. Indeed, due to the scope of their description of the state's natural resources, these two scientists may well be considered the founding fathers of California's geology and botany. It is remarkable that many of these resources still exist, particularly when considered in light of the post's location at the tip of the densely populated San Francisco peninsula. As the surrounding areas have become more intensely urban, the Presidio continues to provide critical refuge for plants and wildlife, as well as for humans who also seek refuge from the hustle and bustle of daily life in the city.

Cattle and horses once trampled the Presidio's fragile native grasses. A salt marsh was filled because it was perceived as "an obstruction to the use of the bay front [and]. . .probably a source of ill health." Running

> "This place and its vicinity has abundant pasturage, plenty of firewood, and fine water, all good advantages for establishing here the presidio or fort which is planned. It lacks only timber, for there is not a tree on all those hills, though the oaks and other trees along the road are not very far away.... Here and near the lake there are *yerba buena* and so many lilies that I almost had them within my tent." —Father Pedro Font, 1776

water was captured for the fast-growing and thirsty city. Even the well-meaning efforts to beautify the post were partially motivated by the desire to "cover the area of sand and marsh waste." Human activities such as building, landscaping, and afforestation led to the fragmentation of natural ecosystems, which threatened coastal dunes, dune scrub, and serpentine grasslands, and drove some plant species to and over the edge of extinction. The Presidio was, after all, an Army base, not an ecological reserve.

The change in mission from military post to national park created an opportunity to apply a modern vision of renewal and value to the evolving landscape. Contemporary restoration goals focus on enhancing natural habitat through the removal of invasive species and their replacement with plants grown at the Presidio's native plant nursery.

Today, ten rare plant communities survive within the Presidio's boundaries and nowhere else in San Francisco. Serpentine grasslands provide habitat where wildflowers and grasses flourish. Sand dunes that once covered vast stretches to the city's edges now are preserved here. The last free-flowing stream in San Francisco, Lobos Creek, runs under oak woodlands to the sea. The geology of the nearby San Andreas fault provides a rich variety of soil and rock substrate fostering botanical diversity. The Presidio is an important resting spot for hawks and other migrating birds as they travel down the Pacific flyway each fall. Some fifty bird species nest on the post and take advantage of the complex mix of natural plant communities, designed landscapes, and planted forests that provide a variety of microhabitats and edge environments.

Because of its resources, the Presidio is a distinctive part of the Central California Coast International Biosphere Reserve, an interna-

Mountain Lake, once the campsite of the Anza Expedition, retains much of its natural beauty, yet human activities have greatly accelerated its evolution from pond to marsh.

(Photograph courtesy Charles Kennard)

tionally significant example of the world's natural regions and one that is easily accessible as a learning laboratory.

Wetlands that once stretched from Fort Point to Fort Mason will be recreated on a portion of Crissy Field, and schoolchildren and adults from the community assist in creating habitat for the Presidio Clarkia (*Clarkia franciscana*) and the Raven's Manzanita (*Arcostaphylos hookeri* ssp. *ravenii*), the last of its kind. There is good reason to hope that the fate of these endangered plants will not be the same as that of the Xerces Blue Butterfly, which in 1949 became the only documented extinction on the Presidio.

THE RAVEN'S MANZANITA LEAF. THIS FEDERALLY ENDANGERED SPECIES OF THE COASTAL PRAIRIE IS FOUND ONLY ON THE PRESIDIO.

(*Photograph ©1994 Middleton/Liittschwager*)

———◇———

LEFT: *LOBOS CREEK, NEAR OUR HOUSE, SAN FRANCISCO, C. 1918.* IN HIS 1985 AUTOBIOGRAPHY, ANSEL ADAMS WROTE, "WITH A RESOLUTE WHISPER, LOBOS CREEK FLOWED PAST OUR HOME ON ITS MILE-LONG JOURNEY TO THE OCEAN. IT WAS BORDERED. . .WITH WATERCRESS AND ALIVE WITH MINNOWS, TADPOLES, AND A VARIETY OF LARVAE. WATER BUGS SKIMMED THE OPEN SURFACES AND DRAGONFLIES DARTED ABOVE THE STREAM BED. IN HEAVY FOG, THE CREEK WAS EERIE, RIPPLING OUT OF NOWHERE AND VANISHING INTO NOTHINGNESS."

(*Photograph © 1995 by the Trustees of the Ansel Adams Publishing Right Trust*)

THE RICHNESS AND BREADTH OF HISTORY AT THE PRESIDIO IS SUGGESTED BY THIS PHOTOGRAPH OF 20TH CENTURY MILITARY POLICE FOLDING THE AMERICAN FLAG NEXT TO 17TH CENTURY CANNON. *(Photograph courtesy Charles Kennard)*

As a park, the Presidio has a longstanding and deeply felt tradition as a place for public recreation.

The Presidio was traditionally an open post, one where civilians were welcome to visit and enjoy the scenery and the military pageantry. In many ways, the public's use of the post as a scenic recreation area paralleled similar uses of Golden Gate Park and Sutro Heights Park as places for interesting and vigorous weekend outings. This public use was institutionalized with the development of a golf course open to civilian members of a private golf club; later, and more democratically, it was reinforced with the establishment of the city's Julius Kahn playground on military land.

The fantastic and elaborate Panama Pacific International Exposition was held in San Francisco in 1915, and many of its state and international pavilions were constructed along the Presidio's northern shoreline. The cooperation and participation of the Army in this great world's fair was enthusiastic and extensive, and soldiers in uniform were admitted free of charge.

Perhaps the deepest-running connection between the Presidio and the concept of public parks, however, lies in the early man-

> "Yesterday...I went to the Presidio, the army reservation where the soldiers live in barracks and in tents. There are beautiful residences where the officers live and a wide cement drive where automobiles and carriages go, with dirt roads for the cavalry.... We saw the stables where the cavalry horses and mules are kept.... They all looked fat and well cared for. We met soldiers on foot, on horseback, and saw them at work at different things. Everyone seemed to be busy about their affairs and everything was so clean and well kept."
>
> — Laura Ingalls Wilder, 1915

agement of the great national parks of California by Presidio soldiers prior to the establishment of the National Park Service. From 1890 to 1914, cavalry troopers rode each summer from San Francisco to Sequoia and Yosemite, where they patrolled the land, established trails, marked boundaries, enforced regulations, and protected resources. These troopers were, in essence, the very first park rangers. The conservation projects they undertook and the example of endurance and public service they set helped establish important precedents for the management of the National Park Service upon its establishment in 1916. Indeed, the ranger uniform and its distinctive flat hat were modeled after the uniform of the soldiers who patrolled the national parks.

The Presidio's role as a park was first written into law in 1972, when the act establishing Golden Gate National Recreation Area declared that the post would be included in the national park if the Army determined it excess to its needs. When the National Park Service assumed stewardship of the Presidio of San Francisco from the U.S. Army in October 1994, it was the continuation of a long, long heritage of mutual cooperation. Considering that its primary mission was not park management, the U.S. Army had been an unusually fine steward of the Presidio's landscape resources.

Now, as a part of the National Park Service, the Presidio offers a rare opportunity to create a great urban park, provide an international center for research and learning, and showcase economically feasible, ecologically sustainable historic preservation.

SOLDIERS AT MEMORIAL DAY CEREMONIES AT THE PRESIDIO'S NATIONAL CEMETERY ARE REMINDERS OF THE PRESIDIO'S MILITARY HERITAGE AND CONNECTIONS TO ITS PAST. *(Photograph courtesy Cindy Ellen Russell)*

TIMELINE

FIRST INHABITANTS

Native Americans are believed to have used the Presidio for fishing, hunting, and both seasonal and permanent occupation. Early signs of their presence include a Crissy Field shell mound and burial site, dated A.D. 740.

SPANISH PERIOD (1769-1821)

1769 Spanish explorers, led by Gaspar de Portola, accidentally discover San Francisco Bay while en route to Monterey Bay.

1775 The first European ship, the *San Carlos*, sails through the Golden Gate into the Bay.

1776 Spanish settlers arrive and establish the Mission San Francisco de Assis.

1794 Indian laborers build Castillo de San Joaquin where Fort Point now stands.

MEXICAN PERIOD (1821-1848)

1821 Mexico gains independence from Spain.

1835 Mexican troops move out of the Presidio to Sonoma barracks.

1846 During the Bear Flag Revolt, John C. Fremont "captures" the Presidio. The U.S. Army takes control of the California.

AMERICAN PERIOD (1848 ONWARD)

1848 The Mexican-American War ends and gold is discovered on the American River.

1850 President Fillmore formally reserves the Presidio "for public purposes." California becomes a state in the Union.

1853 Construction begins on the fort at Fort Point.

1861 The Civil War breaks out. Completed Fort Point receives armament.

1892 Concrete batteries above Fort Point take shape.

1898 The Spanish-American War reshapes territories.

1906 The Great San Francisco Earthquake and fire jolt the city. Presidio troops fight fires, assist in relief activities, and establish refugee camps within the Presidio. Letterman Hospital opens to the public during the disaster.

1915 The Panama-Pacific International Exposition draws crowds to the Marina and along the Presidio shore. General Pershing's house burns.

1914-1918 Europe ignites in World War I.

1921 The Army establishes Crissy Airfield.

1933-1937 The Golden Gate Bridge rises over the entrance to San Francisco Bay and overshadows old Fort Point.

1941-1945 The Presidio serves as a major training center for Army troops headed for the World War II Pacific Theater.

1948 The Army's Coast Artillery School moves to Fort Scott.

1951 The ANZUS Pact and U.S.-Japan Joint Security Pact are signed on the Presidio.

1954 Nike Missile launch site is built.

1964-1973 The "police action" in Vietnam. Southeast Asia-bound troops arrive at and leave from the Presidio.

1970 Fort Point is officially designated as a National Historic Site.

1972 Golden Gate National Recreation Area becomes one of the first and one of the largest urban national parks in the country.

1988 Congress passes the Base Closure Bill and the Presidio is scheduled for decommissioning.

1989 The Loma Prieta earthquake rattles San Francisco, and Presidio troops assist in relief activities.

1990 Planning begins for the transfer of the Presidio from the Army to the National Park Service.

1994 The Sixth Army leaves, and the Presidio officially becomes part of the National Park Service.

(Adapted from The Official Map & Guide to the Presidio of San Francisco)